W9-CCI-278

ANCIENT CIVILIZATIONS

MESOPOTAMIA

COLIN HYNSON

WORLD ALMANAC® LIBRARY

Please visit our web site at: www.worldalmanaclibrary.com
For a free color catalog describing World Almanac® Library's list of high-quality books
and multimedia programs, call 1-800-848-2928 (USA) or 1-800-387-3178 (Canada).
World Almanac® Library's fax: (414) 332-3567.

Library of Congress Cataloging-in-Publication Data

Hynson, Colin.
    Mesopotamia / by Colin Hynson.
      p. cm. — (Ancient civilizations)
    Includes bibliographical references and index.
    ISBN 0-8368-6192-2 (lib. bdg.)
    1. Iraq—Civilization—To 634—Juvenile literature. I. Title.
    DS69.5.H96   2006
    935—dc22   2005051686

This North American edition first published in 2006 by
World Almanac® Library
A Member of the WRC Media Family of Companies
330 West Olive Street, Suite 100
Milwaukee, WI 53212 USA

This U.S. edition copyright © 2006 by World Almanac® Library. Original edition
copyright © 2006 by Hodder Wayland. First published in 2006 by Hodder Wayland,
an imprint of Hodder Children's Books, a division of Hodder Headline Limited,
338 Euston Road, London NW1 3BH, U.K.

Project editor: Kirsty Hamilton
Designer: Simon Borrough
Maps: Peter Bull
World Almanac® Library editor: Gini Holland
World Almanac® Library art direction: Tammy West
World Almanac® Library cover design: Dave Kowalski
World Almanac® Library production: Jessica Morris

Picture credits: Gianni Dagli Orti / Corbis: Title page, contents, pp. 9, 10, 11, 13, 14, 16, 27,
32, 35, 41, 42; Corbis: p. 4; Nick Wheeler / Corbis: p. 6; Archivo Iconografico, S.A./ Corbis:
p. 7; Werner Forman/Corbis: p. 8; The Art Archive / British Museum: p. 12; Topfoto.co.uk:
pp. 15, 30; Charles & Josette Lenars / Corbis: p. 18; The Art Archive / Archaeological Museum
Bagdad / Dagli Orti: p. 19; TopFoto.co.uk © The British Museum /HIP: pp. 20, 22, 23, 24, 25
(right), 26, 31, 43, 44; Barney Burstein / Corbis: p. 21; TopFoto.co.uk, HIP / CM Dixon: pp. 25
(left); Silvio Fiore / Topfoto.co.uk: p. 28; The Art Archive / Archaeological Museum Aleppo
Syria / Dagli Orti: p. 29; The Art Archive / Dagli Orti (A): p. 33; The Art Archive / Musée du
Louvre Paris / Dagli Orti: p. 34; The Art Archive / Archaeological Museum Bagdad / Dagli Orti:
p. 36; David Lees / Corbis: p. 37; The Art Archive / Musée du Louvre Paris / Dagli Orti (A):
p. 38; Michael S. Yamashita / Corbis: p. 39; Topfoto.co.uk © The British Museum / HIP /
Warad–Marduk: p. 40; Stephanie Sinclair / Corbis: p. 45

Printed in China

1 2 3 4 5 6 7 8 9 10 09 08 07 06

ᚾᚾᚾᚾᚾᚾᚾᚾᚾᚾᚾᚾᚾᚾᚾᚾᚾᚾ
CONTENTS

WHO WERE THE MESOPOTAMIANS?

When historians talk about the Mesopotamians, they are not talking about one group of people or one nation. The word *Mesopotamia* means "the land between the rivers." This phrase refers to land in modern-day Iraq, with some small parts in Syria and Turkey. The rivers are the great rivers of the Euphrates and the Tigris. From about 3500 B.C., this land gave rise to some of the earliest civilizations in history. The people in these civilizations were known as the Mesopotamians.

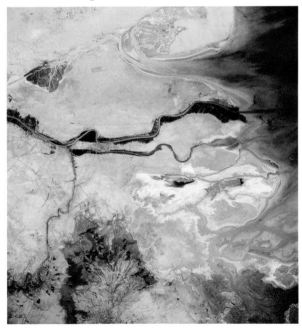

▲ A satellite photograph of present-day Iraq, showing a portion of the Tigris and Euphrates Rivers, which empty into the Persian Gulf.

THE LAND AND CLIMATE

The area of Mesopotamia is dry and hot in summer and much colder in winter, with little rainfall at any time of the year. This dry climate means that anybody who lived in this region in ancient times had to be close to the Euphrates and Tigris Rivers. Both of the rivers flooded every year between the months of April and June. As did their ancient Egyptian neighbors, the Mesopotamians relied on their rivers to flood every year to water and feed their crops. If the floods did not happen, then the people would go hungry. The rivers occasionally changed course and caused floods where they had never been before. When this happened, people had to leave and find a new place to live.

THE MESOPOTAMIAN CIVILIZATIONS

The Mesopotamians were a collection of different civilizations. They formed in what is now the modern Middle East and were centered on the area that is today's Iraq. These civilizations began to arise from 4000 B.C. During the next three thousand years, Mesopotamians created the first urban civilizations; invented things like the wheel, writing,

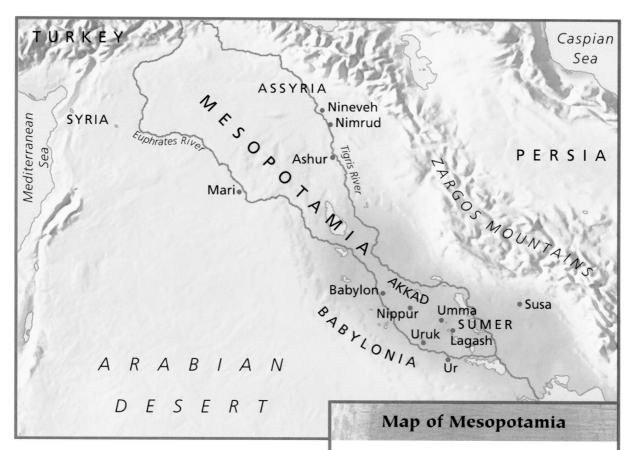

TURKEY

SYRIA

Mediterranean Sea

Euphrates River

MESOPOTAMIA

ASSYRIA

Nineveh
Nimrud

Ashur

Tigris River

Mari

Caspian Sea

PERSIA

ZARGOS MOUNTAINS

Babylon

AKKAD

Nippur

Umma

Susa

BABYLONIA

Uruk

SUMER

Lagash

ARABIAN

DESERT

Ur

Map of Mesopotamia

What does it tell us?

This map shows how Mesopotamia extended between its rivers. Although the whole area does not get much rainfall, the north of Mesopotamia does get more rain than the south. Differences in the amount of rainfall had an impact on the different kinds of civilizations that arose. The lack of rainfall in the south meant it was far more important that farmers who lived there collect the river waters for agriculture. The northern part of Mesopotamia did not have to spend as much time diverting water onto crops. This freed northerners to pursue activities beyond farming.

and number systems; and developed large-scale agriculture. After the fifth century B.C., the Persians, from what is now modern-day Iran, conquered Mesopotamia. This defeat marked the beginning of the end for Mesopotamian civilization, as the Persians imposed their culture on their newly conquered lands.

Many different civilizations arose and fell in Mesopotamia at different periods of history. The dates in which they flourished overlapped, and they shared many characteristics. The major civilizations were the Chaldeans, Akkadians, and the civilizations covered in this book: Babylonian, Sumerian, and Assyrian.

THE SUMERIANS

In about 3000 B.C., a group of people moved from the north of Mesopotamia to an area south of modern-day Baghdad and intermarried with a local people called the Ubaidians. From these two groups arose a new civilization called the Sumerians. The first known ruler of the Sumerians was Etana, King of Kish (c. 2800 B.C.).

In 2300 B.C., the Sumerians were conquered by—and then merged with—the Akkadians. After 2000 B.C., continual struggles for power weakened Sumerian civilization. At the end of this struggle, in 1728 B.C., King Hammurabi became the sole ruler of Sumer. Hammurabi's rise to power marked the end of the Sumerian Empire and the rise of the Babylonians.

Wedding prayer

"Into the Tigris and Euphrates may flood water be brought . . . May the holy queen of vegetables pile high the grain heaps and mounds."

What does it tell us?

This extract from a Babylonian prayer, composed in about 2000 B.C., was said at a wedding. The prayer refers to the flooding of the two rivers and also to the importance of the floods for farming. It was a wedding prayer to invite the married couple to share in the crops that would grow because of the flooded rivers.

The ancient site of Uruk

What does it tell us?

The ancient site of Uruk (*shown here*) was continually occupied for about five thousand years, up until about A.D. 300. The size of the remains that still can be seen shows just how large and important cities became in Mesopotamia. This is just one of several large cities that flourished in Mesopotamia.

THE BABYLONIANS

The Babylonian people occupied land to the south of the city of Baghdad now in modern Iraq. They came to occupy the same land as the previous Sumerian civilization that had begun to fall apart in the eighteenth century B.C. The Babylonian king, Hammurabi, united and strengthened the people of his land in this period. The Babylonians adopted and improved many Sumerian traditions, such their artistic styles and architecture. Babylonian civilization flourished, and their way of life was copied by many of their neighbors. The Babylonian world remained more or less unchanged for the next 1,200 years. It was only in 539 B.C. that the Persians conquered Babylonia.

THE ASSYRIANS

The Assyrians lived in the area of modern-day Iraq that started at about where the modern border between Turkey and Iraq is now and then extended down to near modern Baghdad. This large area controlled by the Assyrians was established by their king Shamsi-Adad I between 1813 and 1780 B.C. By the middle of the eighth century B.C., Assyria had become the most powerful civilization in Mesopotamia.

The Assyrians were seen by other Mesopotamian societies as being warlike and aggressive. To mark their victories and establish the importance of their rule, the kings of Assyria built huge palaces and temples. Many were decorated with stone

Cultivating sugarcane on the bank of the Tigris River

What does it tell us?

This beautifully detailed carving (c. 668–630 B.C.) shows crops growing by the edge of one of the two great rivers of ancient Mesopotamia. The crop that is being harvested is sugarcane, a luxury food that only the most wealthy could afford. The Tigris River is represented by waves, fish, and swimming figures. This carving gives the river as much importance as the crop itself, which shows us how important the rivers were to Mesopotamia's farmers.

reliefs and glazed tiles that show the king participating in state ceremonies. The Assyrian Empire began to fall apart in the sixth century B.C. through a series of civil wars and weak rulers.

HOW WERE THE MESOPOTAMIANS RULED?

The Mesopotamian civilizations are generally seen as the first urban societies in history. As more and more people were drawn to live in cities such as Ur, Babylon, and Ashur, rulers struggled to find ways to control their expanding populations. Large groups of people, competing with one another, often became threats to the established order. The Mesopotamians were continually fighting each other as well as having to deal with foreign invaders.

All Mesopotamian societies promoted order with strong and central leadership. Mesopotamian leaders saw it as desirable for the people to be organized in a highly structured way, in which everyone knew their places and there were no challenges to the rulers.

MESOPOTAMIAN KINGS

Until King Hammurabi became the monarch of Babylon in 1728 B.C., there are very few details about how the Mesopotamians ruled themselves. Nonetheless, archaeologists know that Mesopotamian societies were ruled by kings. They even know the names of the Sumerian kings because, in about 1800 B.C., a "king list" was written down on a clay tablet. The first kings listed were recorded as living for thousands of years, so some of the names and dates on the tablet are questionable. The development of writing and written laws in ancient Mesopotamia means that a great deal

Worshippers led to a king

What does it tell us?

One of the most powerful and important Sumerian kings was Ur-Nammu, who ruled in c. 2112–2095 B.C. This carving (c. 2050 B.C.) shows him on his throne, receiving a goddess. She is leading two bare-headed worshippers to him. Mesopotamian kings were not worshipped as gods, so the image must be telling us something else. Ur-Nammu built many great temples in the city of Ur, and this may show him being thanked for this.

of information exists about individual kings in Sumerian, Assyrian, and Babylonian cultures.

GOD'S REPRESENTATIVES

In both Babylon and Assyria, kings often were seen as divinely chosen. People were told that the main gods chose the kings of these two civilizations, so the people saw kings as ruling in the name of the gods. Ruling with the support of the gods made armed resistance to the king very difficult. Assyrian kings acted as high priests, and Babylonian kings also took an important part in religious rites.

SARGON II

One of the great Assyrian kings was Sargon II. He reigned from about 722–705 B.C. While on the throne of Assyria, he extended his rule over numerous states in what is now Syria and Turkey. He also conquered the ancient kingdom of Israel as far south as Jerusalem. To administer this empire, he created a civil service and appointed governors to rule areas of the empire in his name. Sargon II built a new city to the north of Nineveh named Dur Sharrukin—a city considered a Biblical myth until recent times—and had a new

Naram-Sin in bronze

What does it tell us?

This bronze head (c. 2250 B.C.), believed to be of the Assyrian king Naram-Sin (c. 2254–2218 B.C.), is one of the finest examples of Mesopotamian metal sculpture ever recovered by archaeologists. Naram-Sin was the first to insist that he was not just a god-chosen king but was a god himself. This sculpture shows us what he—the "king of the universe," as he called himself—looked like.

palace built there. Excavated by French scholar Paul Emile Botta, this palace bears carved inscriptions that verify many historical and Biblical events.

HAMMURABI

Hammurabi is one of the best known of the Mesopotamian kings. Hammurabi was king of Babylon between 1728 and 1685 B.C. He built an empire that stretched from the Persian Gulf to the shores of the Mediterranean Sea. Hammurabi became the most powerful king in the region, and Babylon was his most important city. He tried to reign in a way that helped his people, by personally supervising the building of new temples and improving agriculture. He is best remembered for the Code of Hammurabi, a series of laws that governed the lives of his subjects.

▲ The Stela of Hammurabi (eighteenth century B.C.), shows King Hammurabi receiving the law from the seated Sun god, Shamash.

The Code of Hammurabi

"Anum and Enlil named me to promote the welfare of the people, Me, Hammurabi, the devout, god-fearing prince, to cause justice to prevail in the land, to destroy the wicked and the evil, that the strong should not oppress the weak."

What does it tell us?

This quote from King Hammurabi in his Code of Hammurabi tells us that Hammurabi believed his right to rule came from the gods Anum and Enlil. It also shows us that he believed he was king for a reason: to look after his people and rule well and justly.

THE CODE OF HAMMURABI

The Code of Hammurabi was created at some unknown time during Hammurabi's reign. When the code was introduced, it was the first known time that laws were written down and put on public display. In this way, everybody in the city could know the laws of Babylon. Part of the code's job also was to set out the way Babylonian society was supposed to be structured.

Many of the laws that are part of the Code of Hammurabi were designed to protect the most vulnerable and weak members of Babylonian society from the most powerful by making sure that all were equally protected by the law. It laid out what punishments would be given for different crimes. These included penalties for surgeons who carried out unsuccessful operations and fines for neglect in various trades. The punishments for crimes against people and property were based on the idea of "an eye for an eye." The general rule was that, for example, if somebody broke another person's bone, then the offender's punishment would be to have the same bone broken.

▲ Shalmaneser III and King Markud-zakir-shumi greet one another in this detail from a carving from the throne of Shalmaneser III.

BABYLONIAN SOCIETY

Proud kings

"I am Shalmaneser, the legitimate king, the king of the world, the king without rival . . . overlord of all the princes, who has smashed all his enemies as if they were earthenware."

What does it tell us?

Shalmaneser III was an Assyrian king. He reigned from 859–824 B.C. During his reign, the Assyrian Empire continued to expand. Mesopotamian kings often wrote boastful things about themselves to help justify their rule and encourage their people's confidence in them.

The Code of Hammurabi divided Babylonian society into three classes: the *amelu*, the *muskinu*, and the *ardu*. The *amelu* were the ruling class of Babylon, including the king and court, senior government officials, and wealthy professionals. The code does not make it clear who the *muskinu* were. They seem to be landless workers. This does not necessarily mean that they were poor. The *muskinu* and *amelu* were supposed to live separately from each other. The *ardu* were slaves. Slaves were protected under the code. They were allowed to buy their freedom, own property, and even own their own slaves.

HOW DID THE MESOPOTAMIANS EXTEND THEIR RULE?

The fertile plains of Mesopotamia, along with the wealth of the great cities, meant that war was a constant feature of Mesopotamian history as different tribes and states fought for control of these riches. The first record of warfare in the region comes from about 3000 B.C. Images from Uruk and Susa show scenes of fighting and of prisoners of war kneeling in front of kings. From then on, Mesopotamia was

The Royal Standard of Ur

What does it tell us?

This section from the Royal Standard of Ur has images of the Sumerian army. It dates from about 2600–2400 B.C. These pictures detail how professionally dressed the Sumerian soldiers were and what kinds of weapons they had. Both spears and swords are shown being carried into battle. The Royal Standard also reveals the use of horses and chariots— not only for use in battle, but also for transporting weapons.

rarely at peace. Different parts of Mesopotamia fought among themselves for power and territory. Mesopotamians also fought external invaders, such as the Persians.

THE FIRST ARMIES

As the Mesopotamians began to organize into more complex societies, they began to think of better ways to defend themselves. One of the ways of doing this was to form armies. A king named Sargon the Great ruled over the Akkadians from about 2335-2279 B.C. During his reign, he conquered virtually all of Mesopotamia. He was successful not only because opposition never united against him, but also because of the way he organized his army. For the first time, he created an army of full-time soldiers.

Before Sargon the Great, kings created armies from local people they brought together to fight a war and then sent home again when the fighting stopped. Sargon the Great raised an army of about ten thousand permanent soldiers and properly trained and equipped them. Because Sargon had to defeat enemies who defended themselves from behind the walls of cities, he also developed new kinds of weapons for sieges, such as battering rams to knock down city gates.

THE ASSYRIAN EMPIRE

About the end of the tenth century B.C., Assyria began to expand. From 1200 B.C.

onward, however, Assyria continually had to defend itself from outside attack. Assyria did this successfully by building an army that would become known throughout Mesopotamia as one of the most ruthless ever seen. The Assyrian king Tiglath-Pileser III—known as King Pul in the Bible—reigned from 745-727 B.C. and wanted control over all Mesopotamia and beyond. He created a permanent army that was mostly made up of non-Assyrians. He defeated the Babylonians, conquered parts of modern-day Syria and Turkey, and made Israel subject to him. One of the ways he kept rule over these lands was to move entire populations of conquered people to different parts of the empire so they could not get together and rebel against Assyrian rule.

Assyrian chariot

What does it tell us?

This stone carving shows an Assyrian chariot going into battle. It dates from about 800 B.C. The carving confirms that chariots usually were ridden by two soldiers. One soldier had the job of steering the chariot, and the other soldier did the fighting.

WEAPONS AND ARMOR

Early Mesopotamians used weapons that were the same as those they used for hunting, such as spears, clubs, and bows and arrows. From 3000 B.C. onward, they began to make new weapons out of metal, such as swords and axes. They usually made them of copper or bronze. After 2000 B.C., they replaced these soft metals with iron, which made their weapons much stronger.

From 2000 B.C., the Mesopotamians' use of horses in war also began to change. Before this date, they used horses mostly to carry weapons and other equipment. Then, as the idea of a cavalry began to develop, Mesopotamians used horses in battle. Soldiers either rode the horses or

Herodotus quote

"The Assyrians went to war with helmets upon their heads made of brass . . . They carried shields, lances, and daggers, very much like the Egyptians."

What does it tell us?

This quote comes from the fifth century B.C. Greek historian Herodotus. Preserved texts such as this help confirm what kinds of weapons the ancient Assyrians carried with them when they went into battle. Texts are more believable if the information they give is also found on paintings and carvings.

▲ This wall painting (c. 522–486 B.C.), shows an Archer of the Royal Guard of Darius I, King of Persia.

A cavalry charge

What does it tell us?

This relief carving from the ninth century B.C. comes from the palace of Kalhu. The relief helps us understand how Mesopotamian soldiers may have fought on horseback. None of the horses have a saddle or stirrups. The soldiers are shown riding in pairs. The first soldier holds on to both horses, and the second soldier wields his bow and arrow.

drove them as they pulled their chariots. The chariots were fast and light and could carry a maximum of four archers.

To protect themselves, Mesopotamian soldiers usually wore leather or metal helmets on their heads. Their armor was made of tiny pieces of bronze that overlapped each other, like the scales of a fish, and were then sewn onto a tunic.

INVADING MESOPOTAMIA

The states that bordered Mesopotamia remained a threat to the states between the Tigris and Euphrates Rivers. The main rivals of the Mesopotamians came from the east. In about 1500 B.C., in what is now modern-day Iran, the Persian kingdom arose. In 558 B.C., Cyrus the Great took the throne of Persia and began to expand his empire. In 546 B.C., he conquered Lydia, a country in modern-day Turkey. He then turned his sights on Mesopotamia. Cyrus the Great attacked, and, in 539 B.C., he conquered Babylonia.

Mesopotamia remained under Persian rule until 331 B.C., when Alexander the Great of Greece drove the Persians out.

WHAT WAS LIFE LIKE FOR THE MESOPOTAMIANS?

The everyday lives of the average people of Mesopotamia have been difficult to uncover. Relying on written and physical evidence to find out about past civilizations, modern historians and archaeologists have found little evidence of the lives of ordinary people. Archaeologists have uncovered much more evidence on the lives of the wealthy and privileged. Objects that have survived usually were owned by the wealthy and have lasted because they were made of stronger, better materials. Writings about people's lives that have survived are usually about those at the top of Mesopotamian society.

THE LIVES OF MESOPOTAMIAN WOMEN

Lives led by women in Mesopotamian society were strictly defined in terms of their role in the family. Mesopotamian women were seen as daughters, wives, or mothers, and they were very rarely seen outside of the confines of their families. If they were, they tended to be royal women or those with rich and powerful husbands. Mesopotamian women were required to be responsible for their homes. Indeed, not keeping a well-ordered house was seen as a good reason for divorce. One reason we do not know much about Mesopotamian homes may be that, since the home was seen as the woman's domain, those who recorded Mesopotamian life did not believe it was important enough to write about.

WOMEN'S RIGHTS

At no point in Mesopotamian history did men and women have equal rights. From early on in Mesopotamian history, however, women were free to go out to the marketplace, buy and sell goods, borrow and lend money, engage in business, and attend to their husbands' legal matters. Several contracts involving women running their own businesses have been found. Some women, such as the high priestess of the temple of the Goddess Bau, had a lot of power. According to a document from about 2350 B.C., the priestess was in charge of the temple and of the one thousand people who worked there throughout the year.

WOMEN AND THE CODE OF HAMMURABI

Babylonian women had only limited protection under the Code of Hammurabi. Married women could easily be divorced for virtually any reason, including childlessness or even poor household management. All the husband had to do was to say "You are not my wife" and return her dowry (property given by the wife's family to the husband's family when the couple get married). Under the code, any woman who tried to do the same thing could be drowned. A woman could not divorce her husband, but she was able to leave him if she could prove cruelty or if he made a false accusation against her.

Women's rights

"If a woman quarrels with her husband . . . the reasons for her prejudice must be presented. If she is guiltless, and there is no fault on her part, but he leaves and neglects her, then no guilt attaches to this woman: She shall take her dowry and go back to her father's house."

What does it tell us?

This is a part of the Code of Hammurabi. Men were allowed to divorce their wives for the most trivial reasons. This part of the Code shows that women also had permission to no longer live with their husbands if they were falsely accused of something or if they could prove "cruelty." They were not, however, actually allowed to divorce.

A FAMOUS MESOPOTAMIAN WOMAN

Although we have few details of most individual women from ancient Mesopotamia, we do know about one of the best-known women from that time, Enheduanna. She was the daughter of Sargon, the king of the Akkadians. She was the chief priestess of the Moon-god temple in Ur in about 2300 B.C. Enheduanna is now the earliest known female poet in the world. Her poetry about the gods and goddesses was very popular at the time.

INSIDE AN ORDINARY MESOPOTAMIAN HOME

Archaeological evidence shows that ordinary people lived in small, cube-shaped houses. These usually had two floors. On the ground floor, most families had workshops and an area for receiving guests. Their living quarters were on the top floor. They also had open courtyards, where their families could cook, eat, and relax. Few families could afford their own bathrooms and toilets. For those who could buy them, drains that emptied into a nearby river were built. Most houses were built of sun-dried bricks made from mud. These helped keep the houses cool in summer. People sometimes painted their door frames red to ward off evil spirits.

A Mesopotamian palace

What does it tell us?

This picture shows the remains of the palace of Nebuchadnezzar II (630-562 B.C.) in Babylon. Even though it is now in ruins, the picture shows the scale of the palace. It also is known as the site of the Hanging Gardens of Babylon, which the Greek writer Philo called one of the seven wonders of the ancient world. Historians still debate about whether the gardens actually existed or not.

ROYAL RESIDENCES

We have much more evidence about the palace homes of the kings of ancient Mesopotamia. These also were built of sun-dried mud bricks and were two stories high, but the similarities end there. Some of the palaces were huge, with as many as three hundred rooms. These rooms had all sorts of functions, from storing treasure to serving as workshops for craftsmen. Nebuchadnezzar II built the most famous royal palace in Babylon. Many historians believe that, sometime between 630 and 562 B.C., he built the Hanging Gardens at his palace. Plants and trees were planted high up the palace walls and could be seen hanging, or suspended, in midair.

MESOPOTAMIAN FASHION

Only a few fragments of Mesopotamian clothing have survived to the present day. All other information

Statue of a bearded man

What does it tell us?

This statue dates from about 3000 B.C. and comes from Tell Asmar. It is a useful statue because it shows a lot about Mesopotamian fashion. For example, this man is not wearing any shoes. The tunic he is wearing goes up only to his waist. He also has a long beard and long hair at the back. Historians and archaeologists believe he was a wealthy man.

about what Mesopotamian men and women wore comes from sculptures, metalwork, and designs on seals (carved stamps used to mark documents).

Artifacts from about 3000 B.C. show men bare-chested and wearing knee- or ankle-length skirts that tied at the waist. They also show that men wore headbands called *fillets*. Women wore plain, knee-length robes that they draped over their left shoulder, with their right shoulder and arm left uncovered. They also wore shawls that they fastened with pins decorated with beads.

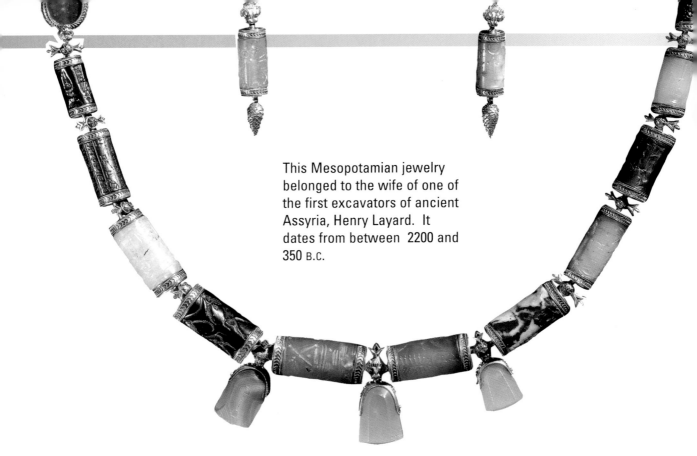

This Mesopotamian jewelry belonged to the wife of one of the first excavators of ancient Assyria, Henry Layard. It dates from between 2200 and 350 B.C.

Artifacts show only small differences between the clothing of rich and poor Mesopotamians. Wealthier Mesopotamians, however, enjoyed wearing clothing with brighter colors and usually added jewelry.

CHANGING FASHIONS

Early Mesopotamians usually made clothing for both men and women from the skins of sheep and goats. Later, they wove cloth from a plant called flax. They found that flax cloth was easy to work into different thicknesses, so they could make different clothes for winter or summer. The clothing worn by both men and women changed very little for several centuries. From about 2300 B.C.,

people began to add decorations to their robes, making them less plain.

One of the Mesopotamian fashions that did change was whether or not men wore beards. Images from 3000 B.C. show all men wearing long beards. One thousand years later, the images changed. Some men still had beards, but others were clean-shaven. Priests are shown without beards and with shaved heads.

MESOPOTAMIAN JEWELRY

Both men and women in Mesopotamia wore earrings and necklaces. During celebrations, they wore even more jewelry. The wealthier Mesopotamians often wore beautiful gold and silver

Gold headddress

What does it tell us?

This gold headdress (c. 2600 B.C.) is named the Sumerian Gold Jewelry of Queen Shub-ad of Ur. It shows us that Mesopotamia had skilled goldsmiths. The gold leaves had to be hammered to the right thickness and then made into the right shapes. A similar headdress was found at the Royal Cemetery at Ur. No one knows whether it was worn by somebody in life or whether it was specially made when the person died so that it could be worn in the coffin.

bracelets and earrings. Their necklaces were set with bright, precious stones, including lapis lazuli and carnelian.

MESOPOTAMIAN METALWORK

Bronze, copper, and tin were common metals in Mesopotamia. They were used to make household goods as well as weapons and parts for chariots. The Mesopotamians are seen by modern historians as skilled metalworkers. Many of the pieces of metal found at the Royal Cemetery of Ur show metalwork of the highest standard of craftsmanship. The gold and silver objects in the cemetery show that the Mesopotamians who worked with these precious metals were as skilled as anyone else in the world at the time. One of the main problems the Mesopotamians faced was that very little metal naturally occurred where they lived. The metals they used had to be brought in from other countries. Experts believe that the gold they used came from what is now modern-day Turkey. Some metals, such as iron and copper, could be found locally.

MESOPOTAMIAN GLASS

One of the greatest achievements of the Mesopotamians was the invention of glass. Most archaeologists believe glass was first created in about 3000 B.C. in Mesopotamia. The earliest objects made from glass were beads. In about 1500 B.C., the Mesopotamians discovered how to make hollow glass vessels, such as bottles and vases. They produced glass until about 1200 B.C., when it mysteriously disappeared. For whatever reason, it did not appear again until about 900 B.C.

Mesopotamian glassware

What does it tell us?

This blue glass bottle comes from the Kassite dynasty and dates from between 1300 and 1200 B.C.. It was found in a grave at Ur. The bottle was made only a few hundred years after the Mesopotamians had learned how to make hollow glass objects. This skill enabled them to make containers that were not only practical but also beautiful. The Mesopotamians also discovered how to color glass. They added cobalt to the molten glass to make a blue color. They used antimony to make white glass and copper to make green glass.

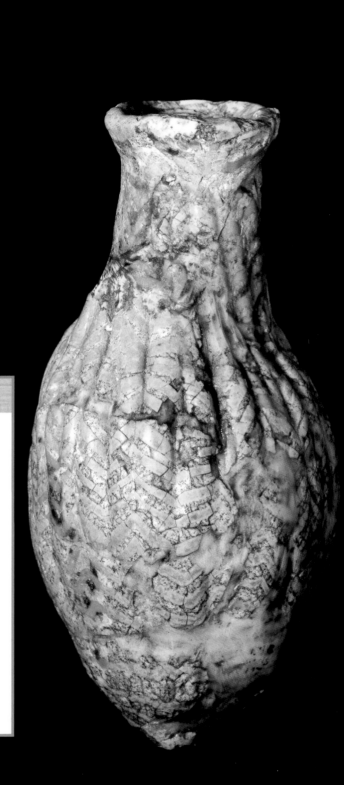

Glazed pottery

What does it tell us?

This piece of Mesopotamian pottery, from about the eighth or seventh century B.C., shows us that Mesopotamians made clay pots on a potter's wheel. It also shows us that the Mesopotamians had learned how to put a glaze on their pots. The glaze made their pots stronger, waterproof, and also decorated the surface. Their earliest glazed pots date from about 1500 B.C. They also used glaze on decorated brickwork.

MESOPOTAMIAN POTTERY

Clay, the main material of pottery, was common in many parts of Mesopotamia. As in many other parts of the ancient world, Mesopotamian potters used their fingers to shape the clay. Evidence shows that, from about 4500 B.C., potters in Mesopotamia began to use wheels that they turned with their legs to make pottery—a method still used today.

WORKING IN STONE

The Mesopotamians also were skilled at carving sculptures. Many of their stone figures are either of gods and goddesses, or of kings and other important people like priests. They also represented ordinary people in these carvings but only to show them serving their king. Mesopotamian carvers were well-known for carving figures in relief. These were flat carvings made of alabaster that could be placed onto walls or gates. They also made statues out of marble and limestone.

Moving a statue

What does it tell us?

This picture—from the wall of the palace of the Assyrian King Sennacherib (704-681 B.C.) at Nineveh—shows us one way that Mesopotamians transported statues. The statue in the picture is not yet finished. Prisoners have placed it on wooden rollers and are shown here pulling it to its destination. The prisoners are being guarded by soldiers who probably have been posted to prevent the prisoners from escaping.

CHILDREN'S TOYS

Excavations by archaeologists at burial sites in Mesopotamia show that Mesopotamian children could enjoy themselves in many ways. Toy animals, wooden balls, and rattles have been found buried at the graves of Mesopotamian children. Toys were only for the children of wealthy people, however. Most children probably had no specially made toys and worked from an early age.

Toy hedgehog

What does it tell us?

This pull-along toy for a Mesopotamian child dates from the twelfth century B.C. The hedgehog is made from limestone, and the cart is made from stone—both strong enough to survive for over three thousand years. Another animal once rode behind the hedgehog. Toys at this time would have been expensive, so only wealthy children had well-made toys. It shows us that children did have toys.

MUSIC

It will never truly be known what Mesopotamian music sounded like in its time, but music played an important part in the Mesopotamians' religious and personal lives. After 2000 B.C., the Sumerians built new temples in their cities. Texts left behind tell us that they sang hymns to their gods in these temples, and that some parts were sung by a priest and others by a choir. Excavations at

The royal lyre

What does it tell us?

This lyre was found in the grave of Queen Pu-abi at the Royal Cemetery at Ur. It dates from about 2600–2400 B.C. and was made from the finest materials, including gold, which would have made it expensive. The fact that this lyre was put in a grave shows us just how important music was to the Mesopotamians.

various tombs have revealed the remains of musical instruments such as flutes, drums, lyres, reed pipes, and harps. The Mesopotamians also were the first people to write down their music and write about how to play the instruments they had.

PLAYING BOARD GAMES

In the 1920s, an English archaeologist named Sir Charles Leonard Woolley excavated some tombs in the ancient Sumerian city of Ur. What he discovered in these royal tombs has helped create a much fuller picture of life in ancient Mesopotamia. Woolley discovered many of Mesopotamia's best-known artifacts, including the Standard of Ur, a decorated box showing scenes of Sumerian life, and

The Royal Game of Ur board

What does it tell us?

This board game is one of the best-known Mesopotamian pieces in the British Museum, London, dating from about 2600 B.C. The main rules for the game were written down in cuneiform in about 177 B.C. and still survive. The rules are complicated, so it is clearly a game for adults. The expensive materials used to make the board and the quality of the workmanship show it could have been used only by somebody with plenty of money.

many of the finest examples of metal-working. Among the treasures he found were two board games. Together, they are called the Royal Game of Ur. The games date from about 2600 B.C. Another simpler board game also has been found at the tomb of Queen Shub-ad, about five hundred miles from Ur. Today, the British Museum Web site has an online version of the Royal Game of Ur.

FARMING AND FOOD

The area of land that the Mesopotamians occupied is part of what is called the "fertile crescent." This land, which curves from Mesopotamia's rivers around to the land along Egypt's Nile River, was one of the first places in the world to be farmed.

Preparing food

What does it tell us?

This detailed stone carving comes from the palace of King Ashurnasirpal (883–859 B.C). It shows a sequence in which servants prepare a meal for the king. It tells us that Mesopotamians were able to prepare complex meals and shows us some of the methods they used. One servant is waving a fan over the food—either to cool it down or to keep flies off the food.

Mesopotamians domesticated animals such as sheep beginning in about 9000 B.C., and they began to grow crops about one thousand years later. As they began to expand their cities, Mesopotamians had to improve their farming methods in order to feed their growing urban populations.

WHAT DID THE MESOPOTAMIANS EAT?

For many Mesopotamians, the most important food was bread. Because they did not grow much wheat, they made most of their bread from barley grains that they ground into flour with huge grinding stones. Mesopotamians added milk, cheese, dried fruit, and seeds to their bread to give it extra flavor. They also used barley to brew a weak beer. They drank this through a straw to avoid any bits of barley that might be floating on the surface of the beer.

Seeds such as lentils, peas, chickpeas, and broad beans were a very important part of the Mesopotamian diet, which they ate either raw or cooked. They also cultivated some seeds, such as alfalfa, for animal fodder. The main vegetables that Mesopotamian farmers grew were leeks,

This ancient Babylonian mill, which was used to grind flour, still stands in modern-day Iraq. ▶

Hunting animals

What does it tell us?

This terra-cotta seal dates from about 2000 B.C. and was found in the city of Mari in modern-day Syria. Although farmers in Mesopotamia raised animals such as goats and sheep, this seal shows they may have looked after animals that usually are not found on a farm. The seal shows deer being tended by a man and a dog. The deer might have been released from the farm to be hunted for sport.

onions, cucumbers, and garlic. Mesopotamians also grew and enjoyed fruits such as apples, figs, pears, and dates. They brought in lettuce and radishes from their neighbors in ancient Egypt.

The Mesopotamians slaughtered farm animals, such as cattle, goats, and sheep, for most of their meat. They also hunted wild game, such as deer. They fished in the Tigris and Euphrates Rivers and in the Mediterranean Sea and Persian Gulf. They considered fish a great delicacy.

MESOPOTAMIAN FARMING

The area of Mesopotamia was so large and variable that farmers in different parts of the region had to develop different ways of growing their crops and caring for their animals. The main differences between regions were varying soil quality and weather in the north and south. In the north, farmers had enough rainfall to water their crops. Southern Mesopotamia received far less rainfall. The Tigris and Euphrates Rivers flooded with runoff from the mountains each

A farmer's instructions

"When you are about to cultivate your field, take care to open the irrigation works so that their water does not rise too high in the field."

What does it tell us?

This instruction to farmers comes from a clay tablet written in about 1700 B.C. The tablet shows us that water collection and storage were very important to Mesopotamian farmers. It also shows us that, with careful irrigation, farmers were able to control the amount of water they let flow on to their fields.

Irrigation canals

What does it tell us?

On the plains of southern Mesopotamia, visitors still can see irrigation canals built thousands of years ago. This picture, from Assur, Iraq, shows us that the canals were a major piece of engineering that required constant maintenance in order to work properly. Some of the canals still are used today.

year between April and June. The floods, unfortunately, did not happen when farmers needed the water most. Therefore, they had to create a way to control and store the water until it was needed. They solved this problem by digging irrigation canals. Mesopotamians designed these canals to channel the flood waters away from the fields. Then they could store the water in these canals until they needed it to water the crops.

These irrigation canals regularly filled up with silt from the rivers, so farmers had to make sure the canals were kept free of silt by digging them out. This duty was important for the whole population because if the canals filled up with silt, then the flood waters would not have enough space to be collected. The water would flood the land at the wrong time, and there would not be enough to water the crops in the heat of summer. Then the crops would fail and there would be famine.

THE GROWING YEAR

In Mesopotamia, the agricultural season began in late October or November when the farmers plowed the land and sowed their seeds. This schedule allowed the seeds to grow in what, for Mesopotamia, was early spring. This is when they most needed the flood water they had stored. They then harvested the ripened crop from the end of April until June.

Cylinder seal showing agricultural statistics

What does it tell us?

This cylinder seal from the Sumerian city of Ur dates from about 2000–1900 B.C. The writing on the seal has a remarkable amount of detail about field sizes, barley yields, and other aspects of farming. Archaeologists have discovered many thousands of these kinds of seals, which tell us that Mesopotamian rulers wanted to record how much food was being produced in their kingdoms. They also give modern archaeologists detailed information about Mesopotamian agriculture.

HOW DID THE MESOPOTAMIANS COMMUNICATE?

One of the great achievements of the Mesopotamians was their invention of writing. Writing meant that all the Mesopotamian civilizations could make much greater progress. Peoples' ideas and decisions could be passed on from one generation to the next and need never be forgotten. Their writing also means that historians can learn much more about the life of the Mesopotamians through their own words. The writings they left behind range from Sumerian lists of crops and the laws of the Babylonians to ancient stories, prayers, and myths.

Cuneiform writing

What does it tell us?

This Sumerian clay tablet, with a tally of sheep, is an example of the cuneiform script. Many of these tablets were put inside a second clay case to make sure the contents of the tablets were not interfered with before the message reached the hands of the person who was supposed to receive it. The text itself would either be read from the left to right or from top to bottom. This depended on which way the scribe wrote the cuneiform text.

WRITING WITH PICTURES

As with other early civilizations, the first kind of writing the Mesopotamians used had pictures to represent a word. These symbols are called *pictographs*. A picture of a fish meant one fish. If a fish had two circles next to it, then it meant two fishes. This kind of writing was usually used by farmers to keep records of their animals and crops. Pictographs were limited because they could be used only to write about objects. This way of writing also meant that Mesopotamians had to memorize a lot of pictographs in order to read and write properly. They could not just put letter sounds together.

A king's necklace bead

What does it tell us?

This necklace bead dates from about 2500 B.C. and belonged to Mesanepada, the King of Hur Mari. The scratches on the surface of the bead are cuneiform inscriptions. This bead shows us that it was not just clay tablets that were used for writing. Any hard surface could be used as well. Here the cuneiform words were scratched or carved rather than pressed into soft material such as clay.

WRITING WITH SYMBOLS

A new way of writing was created by the Sumerians in about 3000 B.C. The pictures of objects were replaced with symbols for each word, allowing written words for things that were not objects and making it possible for words in the Sumerian language to be written. This kind of writing is known as *phonographs*.

WRITING WITH LETTERS

Between 1700 B.C. and 1500 B.C., the world's first alphabet was developed in ancient Palestine and Syria. In an alphabet, one symbol or letter represents one sound rather than an entire word. Alphabetic writing is simpler to read than earlier forms, because people only need to learn the symbols for the small number of sounds that make up words rather than memorize a large number of unique symbols. By about 1000 B.C., the Mesopotamians began to create their own alphabet—different from the one created in Palestine and Syria—using a form of cuneiform writing.

The Code of Hammurabi

What does it tell us?

Mesopotamian rulers wrote their laws down so that everybody could read them. This picture shows the block of black basalt stone into which the Code of Hammurabi was carved in the eighteenth century B.C. The stone is over 6 feet (2 meters) tall and weighs about 4 tons. This stone shows how Babylonian laws were communicated to the people. People who could read were asked to call out what was written on the stone.

WRITING ON CLAY

The Mesopotamians did not write on paper or even on papyrus, as the ancient Egyptians did. They wrote on soft clay tablets. They did this by holding a piece of soft clay in one hand. They flattened the top of the clay and then wrote the words by pressing a stylus into the clay to leave a mark. The stylus usually was made from the stem of a water reed. When they finished writing, the people dried the clay, and the writing became permanent. When cities were burned during wars, these tablets often were baked hard enough to last for thousands of years. The characters written on this kind of tablet looked like a series of wedge-shaped marks. This kind of writing is known as *cuneiform*, which comes from the Latin word for "wedge." Wedge-shaped letters were easier for people to carve into stone than curved letters. Cuneiform was used to inscribe the Code of Hammurabi onto blocks of stone, preserving this law.

CYLINDER SEALS

One of the ways that Mesopotamians communicated with each other was by printing with cylinder seals. These seals were invented in about 3500 B.C. in southern Mesopotamia. They were about 1 inch (3 cm) long. Merchants often used cylinders to mark their goods and to record agreements between themselves. They carved cuneiform words and pictures into the surface of the seal and carried them on a string or a pin. The seals were then rolled out onto soft clay tablets to leave a continuous impression. Mesopotamians usually made these seals of stone, but they could also be bone, shell, ivory, wood, or metal.

Cylinder seals

What does it tell us?

This Uruk seal (c. 4000-2000 B.C.) shows how all cylinder seals worked. The seal was placed on a piece of soft clay and then rolled over it. When the seal was taken off, it left behind an impression of the image that had been carved into the cylinder. Because it could be used over and over, it was an ancient way of printing written work, rather than having to carve each word or picture by hand.

WHO DID THE MESOPOTAMIANS WORSHIP?

The Mesopotamians worshipped many different gods and goddesses. Belief in many different gods and goddesses is known as polytheism. These gods and goddesses had different names in different cities. Their names also changed over time. The main god of Babylon was Marduk. The people of the city of Ashur had a god called Ashur. People in cities chose one of these gods to be their special *city god*.

SOME SUMERIAN GODS

The Sumerians had four major gods, who were known as the creating gods. These gods were An, the god of heaven; Ki, the goddess of Earth; Enlil, the god of air; and Enki, the god of water. Heaven, earth, air, and water were seen as the main elements that made up everything in the universe.

Below these gods were some lesser deities, including three sky gods and goddesses. These were Nanna, the god of the moon; Utu, the god of the Sun; and Innana, the queen of heaven. Innana also was the goddess of love and war.

Making an offering

What does it tell us?

This limestone plaque dates from about 2500–2300 B.C. It comes from the southern Mesopotamian city of Ur and shows a religious procession in progress. It reveals information about religious processions and festivals in Mesopotamia, such as how the people presented offerings. In both tiers of this plaque, a person is giving the seated gods an offering, probably of cloth, as a form of worship to the gods.

Below these lesser deities, many minor gods and goddesses ruled. These included gods for rivers and mountains, fields and farms, and even gods of such tools as axes, plows, and brick molds.

WORSHIPPING GODS

The Mesopotamians believed that the gods and goddesses played an active part in their everyday lives, as did many other ancient peoples. All the major Mesopotamian civilizations—from Sumerian, to Babylonian, to Assyrian—believed it was important to worship the gods on a regular basis, particularly when asking for something.

Much of the worship took place in the temples, with priests leading. The priests composed hymns to praise the gods and goddesses and to thank them for what they already had done. Both the priest and any worshippers in the temple usually sang these hymns.

Praying statues

What does it tell us?

These Sumerian statues (c. 2700 B.C.) come from the Square Temple at Eshnunna. They are meant to represent people praying. The fact that they were found at a temple tells us they were probably left as offerings. Experts believe the statues were left to pray perpetually once the worshippers had left the temple.

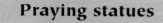

RELIGIOUS FESTIVALS

During the year, the Mesopotamians set aside certain days as special holy days or festivals. During the city festivals, the city gods and goddesses were praised. In return, worshippers hoped the gods and goddesses would protect them and the their cities. Many of these festivals were linked to important times in the farming calendar. One example of this was the festival of *akitu*, which was a time to thank the gods for the important barley harvest.

TEMPLES

Temples could be found in every town and city in Mesopotamia. In the larger

Statue of Gilgamesh

What does it tell us?

The *Epic of Gilgamesh* is one of the best-known stories to come out of Mesopotamia. The Sumerians wrote the stories down in about 2000 B.C. This statue of Gilgamesh dates from about 800 B.C., more than one thousand years later. The date of the statue tells us the Mesopotamians treasured this story throughout their long history.

and more important cities, people could worship the gods and goddesses in several temples. There always was one temple, however, that was more important than all of the others. This was the temple in which people worshipped the god that protected the city. For example, the Sumerian city of Lagash had a temple built to their city goddess, Baba.

THE TEMPLE BUILDING

Temples in Mesopotamia were not thought of just as places where people went to worship and to make offerings to the gods. People believed the gods actually lived in the temples. The temples also contained rooms for the priests, courtyards for public worship, and storage areas for valuables such as gold, jewelry, and barley. Barley was one of the most important crops in Mesopotamia because it was used to make both bread and beer. A high wall surrounded the entire temple to separate it from the rest of the city.

THE ZIGGURAT

The best-known type of Mesopotamian temple was a temple tower called a *ziggurat*. The word ziggurat comes from an Assyrian word meaning "pinnacle." Archaeologists have excavated sixteen ziggurats, all built between 4000 B.C. and 600 B.C., and they know about others from various texts that describe them. Ziggurat ruins still stand at Ur, Uruk, and Nippur.

The structure of these ziggurats followed a common pattern. They are pyramid-shaped, with several flat platforms built on top of each other. At the top of the ziggurat sits a temple. A solid structure with no rooms or passages inside, the pyramid has steps on the outside that lead to the top. The most famous ziggurat was built in Babylon and was dedicated to the god Marduk. This ziggurat inspired the story of the Tower of Babel that is mentioned in the Bible.

The ziggurat at Ur

What does it tell us?

This ziggurat in the ancient city of Ur, known today as Tell al-Muqayyar, dates from about 2000 B.C. The British archaeologist, Sir Charles Leonard Woolley, reconstructed it in the 1920s and 1930s to show it as it would have looked when it was first built. His reconstruction shows us how a ziggurat was designed. Separate levels were built on top of each other, and the temple was placed on the top. The long staircases may have played an important part in religious processions because they could have accommodated a long line of people.

DEMONS AND MONSTERS

The Mesopotamians did not just believe in the existence of gods and goddesses; they also believed in demons, spirits, ghosts, and other supernatural beings.

These demons took on many forms, usually a mixture of human and animal. They also took on the personalities of people and animals. One of the most common demonic images is of a man with wings or with an eagle head or a

A prayer

"From the land of the rising to the land of the setting sun.
O mountain, Lord of life, you are indeed Lord!
O Bel of the lands, Lord of life you yourself are Lord of life.
O mighty one, terrible one of heaven, you are guardian indeed!
O Bel, you are Lord of the gods indeed!"

What does it tell us?

This prayer dates from about 1600 B.C. What it shows us is that when Mesopotamians prayed, they did not always ask for something from the gods. Various writings tell us that the Mesopotamians believed the gods had to be praised both before and after praying for favors. This prayer is directed to the god Bel.

cloak made of fish. People believed the demons were responsible for all sorts of misfortunes. The Mesopotamians also believed they needed to pray to the gods to avoid the demons and be protected from their evil.

MESOPOTAMIAN MYTHOLOGY

The most famous Mesopotamian myth is the *Epic of Gilgamesh*. Written in cuneiform on twelve clay tablets about 2000 B.C., it tells the story of a Babylonian king who lived in about 2700 B.C., called Gilgamesh (*see page 38*). His subjects prayed to be released from his oppressive rule. The gods sent a wild man called Enkidu to fight Gilgamesh. The fight ended in a draw, and the two of them became friends who shared many adventures. They returned to Gilgamesh's palace, where Enkidu died, and Gilgamesh left to find a plant that would give him eternal youth. He lost the plant to a serpent and returned to his home to end his days.

A statue of the demon Pazuzu ▶ (c. 700 B.C.) shows his winged human form and animal-like face.

WHAT DID THE MESOPOTAMIANS CONTRIBUTE TO THE WORLD?

The Mesopotamian civilizations have left behind a legacy that remains with us today. Many of their stories and buildings have similarities with stories and buildings in the Bible. For example, the story of Ut-napishtim is about the world being deluged in a great flood. Also, the main temple in Babylon may be the source for the Tower of Babel. Some scholars think the three wise men from the East who traveled to Bethlehem may have been Mesopotamian astronomers.

Remarkably, three main areas of Mesopotamian achievement are still with us today. These are transportation, mathematics, and astronomy.

TRANSPORTATION

The Mesopotamians also have been credited with inventing one of the most important objects in history: the wheel. The first wheels appeared in ancient Mesopotamia in about 3000 B.C. They were solid wheels that were made from

Wheeled transportation

What does it tell us?

This model of a chariot comes from the city of Ur and dates from about 2000 B.C. It tells us about the design and shape of chariots in Mesopotamia at this time. The driver had a seat in front, and he could use the area at the back to transport goods. The wheels are solid rather than made with spokes. Because spokes came later, this helps historians figure out when the model was made.

What does it tell us?

This granite weight in the shape of a duck dates from about 2000 B.C. It comes from Ur at a time when the city was becoming more powerful. These weights have been found throughout the city. This shows us that weighing and measuring in Ur was becoming standardized: Everyone used the same ways to weigh and measure things. This weight is 2 talents. A talent is about 66 pounds (30 k) and is divided into 60 units called *minas*.

several wooden planks. These planks were shaped into discs and held together with metal bands. About one thousand years later, people began to use wheels with spokes. Mesopotamians had to create roads between towns and cities. Wheels and roads made communication quicker and easier, and allowed armies to move around quickly. A major advance for human civilization, much of modern life would not exist without the wheel, a key part of machines and transportation.

MATHEMATICS

When Mesopotamians invented writing, they also created a way of recording their numbers. Because writing was first used by farmers to keep a record of the amount of grain they grew or how many cattle they kept, they also needed numbers to keep their accounts.

The Mesopotamians had two ways of counting. The first one was based on counting in units of sixty: a sexagesimal system of counting. We still use this way of counting. When we measure time, we count in sixties. There are sixty seconds in a minute and sixty minutes in an hour. In mathematics, we still divide a circle into 360 parts called degrees: 360 is a multiple of 60 (6 x 60 = 360). Dividing the day into twelve daytime and twelve nighttime hours is another invention from Mesopotamia.

The other method of Mesopotamian counting was based on what is called

Astronomical tablet

What does it tell us?

This astronomical tablet comes from the Royal Palace of Nineveh about 700 B.C. Along with written observations of events in the night sky, it also charts the future movements of the stars and planets. This tells us that the priests were able to record what they saw in the sky and then believed they could work out what would happen in several months' or years' time.

the decimal system. This method of counting is based on tens, hundreds, and thousands. The decimal system is the main number system used today.

ASTRONOMY

Mesopotamian priests observed the night sky carefully and made precise notes about the positions of planets and stars and the phases of the moon. They believed that the positions of the planets and stars could act as omens. In about 500 B.C., the priests divided the night sky into twelve equal parts and grouped the stars in each of these parts into patterns called constellations. From these twelve divisions of the night sky, the modern zodiac, the basis for star signs and horoscopes, was developed.

MODERN MESOPOTAMIA

Mesopotamia is now modern-day Iraq. The Mesopotamian civilization declined with their defeat at the hands of the Persian king, Cyrus the Great, in 539 B.C. In 331 B.C., Alexander the Great, the

Macedonian king of Greece, conquered the entire region, officially ending the ancient Mesopotamian civilization. The area then was conquered by the Arabs in A.D. 638, and the people converted to the Muslim faith. It later was controlled either by conquering Mongols or Turkey until the end of World War I in 1918. After being briefly ruled by Britain, Iraq achieved independence in 1921. Unrest festered inside the country from the 1950s until the end of the 1970s, when Saddam Hussein took power.

Saddam Hussein's Iraq fought a war with Iran and invaded the neighboring state of Kuwait. In 2003, a coalition army, led by the United States and Great Britain, invaded Iraq and overthrew the government of Saddam Hussein. Despite the destruction of many of the country's ancient treasures during this last war, modern Iraqis continue to honor the contribution their Mesopotamian heritage has made to their culture and to the world—from the wheel to myths to mathematics.

Modern Mesopotamian palace

What does it tell us?

Saddam Hussein built an enormous palace in the 1980s. Four stories high and shaped like a ziggurat, he had it built next to King Nebuchadnezzar II's old palace. This palace shows us how much influence Mesopotamian civilization still has on modern-day Iraq. Over the years, Iraqi leaders have wanted to show the people they ruled that they could be as strong as ancient Mesopotamian kings.

TIME LINE

All dates are B.C.

4000 First civilizations arise in Mesopotamia

3000 Writing developed in Mesopotamia with Sumerian *phonographs*

3000 Wheel is invented in Mesopotamia

2800 Etana, first known ruler of the Sumerians, takes the throne

2335 Sargon the Great, the Assyrian king, comes to the throne of Akkadians

2200 Akkadian rule of Mesopotamia declines

2000 *Epic of Gilgamesh* written down; ziggarat at Ur built

1728 Hammurabi becomes king of Babylon, ending Sumerian rule

1000 Mesopotamians develop their own alphabet

630 Nebuchadnezzar II starts his reign in Babylon

539 Persians conquer Babylonia in Mesopotamia

331 Mesopotamia taken over by Alexander the Great, ending the ancient Mesopotamian civilization

FIND OUT MORE

BOOKS

Gambino, Elena. *Ancient Mesopotamians.* Peter Bedrick, 2000.

Greene, Jacqueline Dembar. *Slavery in Ancient Egypt and Mesopotamia.* Sagebrush, 2001.

Moss, Carol. *Science in Ancient Mesopotamia.* Franklin Watts, 1999.

Reade, Julian. *Mesopotamia.* British Museum Press, 2000.

Roaf, Michael. *Cultural Atlas of Mesopotamia and the Ancient Near East.* Checkmark Books, 1990.

Zeman, Ludmila. *The Last Quest of Gilgamesh.* Tundra Books, 1998.

WEB SITES

www.mesopotamia.co.uk/menu.html
Explore the main civilizations of Mesopotamia with this interactive British Museum site.

www.fordham.edu/halsall/ancient/asbook.html
Click on the word *Mesopotamia* to learn more about writings from ancient Mesopotamia.

http://oi.uchicago.edu/OI/MUS/ED/TRC/MESO/
Try out this Oriental Institute of the University of Chicago site by going to their "Kids Corner."

http://www.crystalinks.com/meso.html
Learn more about the fertile crescent.

GLOSSARY

Akkadia—a region of Mesopotamia in the south of modern-day Iraq

Akkadians—people who lived near modern-day Baghdad and whose main city was Agade, which was founded by King Sargon in about 233 B.C.

amelu—the Babylonian ruling class

ardu—Babylonian slaves

artifacts—human-made creations of a culture—from works of art to household goods—that provide evidence of that culture or period of time from which they come

Assyria—region of Mesopotamia in the north of modern-day Iraq

Babylon—region of Mesopotamia in the south of modern-day Iraq

carnelian—a red stone that can be cut and polished and used in jewelry

Chaldeans—sometimes called the Neo-Babylonians, this group came from southern Mesopotamia, ruled Babylonia from 612 B.C., and lost their empire to the Persians in 539 B.C.

cuneiform—style of writing used by the Mesopotamians, which involved making marks in soft clay with a wedge-shaped instrument. The word *cuneiform* comes from the Latin word for "wedge"

cylinder seal—tube, bead, or other cylinder engraved with a design and then rolled over soft clay to leave an impression behind

decimal system—ancient number system, used worldwide today, based on units of ten

king list—a text recording the names of kings and the lengths of their reigns; the most famous king list comes from Sumer

lapis lazuli—a deep-blue, semi-precious gemstone often used in Mesopotamian jewelry

law codes—texts recording various crimes and the penalties attached to them; the most famous code was the legal *Code of Hammurabi*

muskinu—landless workers in Babylon

sexagesimal—a number system based on units of sixty, still used in telling time, in geometry, and in other mathematical applications

stela—a stone pillar or slab, usually carved or incised, which was used to commemorate an event

Sumer—a region of Mesopotamia in the south of modern-day Iraq

talent—an ancient unit of weight equal to about 66 pounds (30 kilograms), which could be divided into 60 smaller units called *minas*

ziggurat—a pyramid-shaped structure with a temple built on the top

INDEX